Published by Palphot Ltd. © Copyright reserved
10, Hahagana St., Herzlia, Israel.
Tel: 972-9-9525252; Fax: 972-9-9525277
Email: palphot @inter.net.il

ISBN 965-280-101-1

Photography:
W. Balke: p.6,14,18,22,28,36,44,52,54,56,60,62,
66,68,70,84,86, 94-95
Garo Nalbandian: p.8,10,12,22,24,26,30,32,34,38,
42,58,72,74,76,80,82,88-89.
Duby Tal & Moni Haramaty: p.50-51,56.
Abrams: p.16.
A. Shabataev: p.20.
L. Borodulin: p.40,64.
R. Nowitz: p.78.

Scripture taken from the HOLY BIBLE. NEW
INTERNATIONAL VERSION. Copyright 1973,
1978,1984 International Bible Society. Used by
permission of Zondervan Bible Publisher's."

We are grateful to Winfried Balke and the
Finnish Bible Society for his invaluable
assistance and inspiration in the preparation
of this book.

The most beautiful Psalms

Palphot

Introduction

The Psalms are central to the Bible, and some of its verses are among the most famous of the Holy Scriptures. Many of us can quote verses, or even entire psalms, by heart. What a treasure we then carry in our hearts! For these Hymns of Praise (the literary translation of the Hebrew "Tehilim") are directed from the innermost part of the heart to the one, almighty God. They address the Lord God, who invites us to pour out our hearts before Him, indeed, who yearns for us to come to Him like children. There are Psalms in which we feel from within how the person who is praying is crying out to his Creator out of deep need, desolation, distress, fear or danger, and clings to Him because human help does not suffice. And together with him we experience how, through prayer, the focus is restored towards the goodness of God and His omnipotence.

Thus the Psalms can, and should, help us realize this and enable us to speak to our Heavenly Father and sense how He wants to change our hearts. We can read the words of the Psalmist literally, or let the words inspire us to express our wishes before God in our own words, with the same openheartedness.

Many Psalms tell of the great deeds of the Lord, Creator of heaven and earth. They praise His magnificent creation, and also the wonderful guidance of His people. We, too, marvel that God has chosen the people of Israel as His people and keeps to His choice.

What He promises, He will surely fulfil.

In the Psalms we learn about the nature of the Lord and are led into praise of His love, omnipotence and gentleness. But we must also acknowledge - as does the author of the Psalms - that we are full of guilt and in dire need of God's mercy. Let us again and again, through the forgiveness we are granted, be permeated with a happy, grateful Halleluya, as it sounds out from many Psalms!

Often, prayers from the Bible sing praises to the beauty of Israel, especially Jerusalem. Zion is set before our eyes as the city that the Lord of Hosts has chosen as His dwelling-place. We must constantly remind ourselves that the Creator of the entire Universe - our Lord - is the God of Abraham, Isaac and Jacob, and that we are therefore intimately connected in a special way with Israel and with its capital Jerusalem. God's plan for salvation is intimately connected with Jerusalem.

So which photographs could better visually complement the chosen verses from the Psalms than pictures from Israel! It is the land that the Lord of history promised and gave to His people Israel, and to which He has led them after almost 2000 years of dispersion since 1948 and particularly in the past few years. It is the Land which the prophet Isaiah envisioned in his words:

And many peoples shall go and say, Come ye, and let us go up to the mountain of the Lord, to the house of the God of Jacob, so He may teach us his ways and we will walk his paths: for out of Zion shall go forth the law and the word of the Lord from Jerusalem (Isaiah 2:3).

Lift up your heads, O you gates;
be lifted up, you ancient doors,
that the King of glory may come in.
Who is the King of glory?
The Lord strong and mighty,
the Lord mighty in battle.
Lift up your heads, O you gates,
lift them up, you ancient doors,
that the King of glory may come in.
Who is he, this King of glory?
The Lord Almighty –
he is the King of glory.

Psalm 24, 7-10

Lord, you have assigned me my
portion and my cup;
you have made my lot secure.
The boundary lines have fallen for me
in pleasant places;
surely I have a delightful inheritance.
I will praise the Lord, who counsels me;
even at night my heart instructs me.
I have set the Lord always before me.
Because he is at my right hand,
I will not be shaken.
Therefore my heart is glad
and my tongue rejoices;
my body also will rest secure,
because you will not abandon me to the grave,
nor will you let your Holy One see decay.
You have made known to me the path of life;
you will fill me with joy in your presence,
with eternal pleasures at your right hand.

Psalm 16, 5-11

Shout with joy to God, all the earth!
Sing the glory of his name;
make his praise glorious!
Say to God: How awesome are your deeds!
So great is your power
that your enemies cringe before you.
All the earth bows down to you,
they sing praise to you,
they sing praise to your name.

Psalm 66, 1-4

All the days ordained for me
were written in your book
before one of them came to be.
How precious to me are your thoughts, O God!
How vast is the sum of them!
Were I to count them,
they would outnumber the grains of sand.

Psalm 139, 16–18

Blessed is the man who does not
walk in the counsel of the wicked
or stand in the way of sinners
or sit in the seat of mockers.
But his delight is in the law of the Lord,
and on his law he meditates day and night.
He is like a tree planted by streams of water,
which yields its fruit in season,
and whose leaf does not wither.
Whatever he does prospers.
Not so the wicked!
They are like chaff
that the wind blows away.
Therefore the wicked will not stand
in the judgment,
nor sinners in the assembly
of the righteous.
For the Lord watches over the way
of the righteous,
but the way of the wicked will perish.

Psalm 1

Blessed are they whose ways are blameless,
who walk according to the law of the Lord.
Blessed are they who keep his statutes
and seek him with all their heart.
They do nothing wrong;
they walk in his ways.
You have laid down precepts
that are to be fully obeyed.
Oh, that my ways were steadfast
in obeying your decrees!
Then I would not be put to shame
when I consider all your demands.
I will praise you with an upright heart,
as I learn your righteous laws.
I will obey your decrees;
do not utterly forsake me.

Psalm 119, 1-8

Give ear to my words, O Lord,
consider my sighing.
Listen to my cry for help,
my King and my God,
for to you I pray.
In the morning, O Lord,
you hear my voice;
in the morning I lay my requests before you
and wait in expectation.

Psalm 5, 1-3

Where can I go from your Spirit?
Where can I flee from your presence?
If I go up to the heavens, you are there;
if I make my bed in the depths, you are there.
If I rise on the wings of the dawn,
if I settle on the far side of the sea,
even there your hand will guide me,
your right hand will hold me fast.
If I say: 'Surely the darkness will hide me
and the light become night around me',
even the darkness will not be dark to you;
the night will shine like the day,
for darkness is as light to you.

Psalm 139, 7-12

As for man, his days are like grass,
he flourishes like a flower of the field;
the wind blows over it and it is gone,
and its place remembers it no more.
But from everlasting to everlasting
the Lord's love is with those who fear him,
and his righteousness with their children's children –
with those who keep his covenant
and remember to obey his precepts.

Psalm 103, 15–18

But I am like an olive tree
flourishing in the house of God.
I trust in God's unfailing love
for ever and ever.
I will praise you for ever
for what you have done;
in your name I will hope,
for your name is good.
I will praise you in the presence
of your saints.

Psalm 52, 8-9

For who is God besides the Lord
And who is the Rock except our God?
It is God who arms me with strength
and makes my way perfect.
He makes my feet like the feet of a deer;
he enables me to stand on the heights.
He trains my hands for battle,
my arms can bend a bow of bronze.
You give me your shield of victory,
and your right hand sustains me;
you stoop down to make me great.
You broaden the path beneath me,
so that my ankles do not turn.

Psalm 18, 31–36

God is our refuge and strength,
an ever-present help in trouble.
Therefore we will not fear,
though the earth give way
and the mountains fall
into the heart of the sea.

Psalm 46, 1-2

You care for the land and water it;
you enrich it abundantly.
The streams of God are filled with water
to provide the people with grain,
for so you have ordained it.
You drench its furrows
and level its ridges;
you soften it with showers
and bless its crops.
You crown the year with your bounty,
and your carts overflow with abundance.

Psalm 65, 9-11

The eyes of all look to you,
and you give them their food at the proper time.
You open your hand
and satisfy the desires of every living thing.

Psalm 145, 15-16

He makes springs pour water into the ravines;
it flows between the mountains.
They give water to all the beasts of the field;
the wild donkeys quench their thirst.
The birds of the air nest by the waters;
they sing among the branches.
He waters the mountains from his upper chambers;
the earth is satisfied by the fruit of his work.

Psalm 104, 10-13

Praise the Lord!
Praise the Lord from the heavens,
praise him in the heights above.
Praise him, all his angels,
praise him, all his heavenly hosts.
Praise him, sun and moon,
praise him, all you shining stars.
Praise him, you highest heavens
and you waters above the skies.
Let them praise the name of the Lord,
for he commanded and they were created.
He set them in place for ever and ever;
he gave a decree that will never pass away.

Psalm 148, 1-6

The day is Yours, and Yours also the night;
You established the sun and moon.
It was You who set all the boundaries of the earth;
You made both summer and winter.

Psalm 74, 16-17

By the word of the Lord
were the heavens made,
their starry host by the breath of his mouth.
He gathers the waters of the sea into jars;
he puts the deep into storehouses.
Let all the earth fear the Lord
let all the people of the world revere him.
For he spoke, and it came to be;
he commanded, and it stood firm.

Psalm 33, 6-9

Shout for joy to the Lord all the earth.
Worship the Lord with gladness;
come before him with joyful songs.
Know that the Lord is God.
It is he who made us, and we are his;
we are his people, the sheep of his pasture.
Enter his gates with thanksgiving
and his courts with praise;
give thanks to him and praise his name.
For the Lord is good
and his love endures forever;
his faithfulness continues
through all generations.

Psalm 100

Come, let us sing for joy to the Lord;
let us shout aloud to the Rock of our salvation.
Let us come before him with thanksgiving
and extol him with music and song.
For the Lord is the great God,
the great King above all gods.

Psalm 95, 1-3

Mount Zion rejoices,
the villages of Judah are glad
because of your judgments.
Walk about Zion, go around her,
count her towers,
consider well her ramparts,
view her citadels,
that you may tell of them
to the next generation.
For this God is our God for ever and ever;
he will be our guide even to the end.

Psalm 48, 11–14

I rejoiced with those who said to me,
Let us go to the house of the Lord.
Our feet are standing in your gates,
O Jerusalem.
Jerusalem is built like a city
that is closely compacted together.
That is where the tribes go up,
the tribes of the Lord,
to praise the name of the Lord
according to the statute
given to Israel.
There the thrones for judgment stand,
the thrones of the house of David.
Pray for the peace of Jerusalem:
May those who love you be secure.
May there be peace within your walls
and security within your citadels.
For the sake of my brothers and friends,
I will say, Peace be within you.
For the sake of the house of the Lord our God,
I will seek your prosperity.

Psalm 122

Praise the Lord,
all you servants of the Lord
who minister by night in the house of the Lord.
Lift up your hands in the sanctuary
and praise the Lord.
May the Lord, the Maker of heaven and earth,
bless you from Zion.

Psalm 134

The Lord is my strength and my song;
he has become my salvation.
Shouts of joy and victory
resound in the tents of the righteous:
The Lord's right hand has done mighty things!
The Lord's right hand is lifted high;
the Lord's right hand has done mighty things!"
I will not die but live,
and will proclaim what the Lord has done.
The Lord has chastened me severely,
but he has not given me over to death.
Open for me the gates of righteousness;
I will enter and give thanks to the Lord.

Psalm 118, 14-19

The righteous will flourish like a palm tree,
they will grow like a cedar of Lebanon;
planted in the house of the Lord,
they will flourish in the courts of our God.
They will still bear fruit in old age,
they will stay fresh and green,
proclaiming, The Lord is upright;
he is my Rock,
and there is no wickedness in him.

Psalm 92, 12-15

Give thanks to the Lord, for he is good.
His love endures for ever.
Give thanks to the God of gods.
His love endures for ever.
Give thanks to the Lord of lords,
His love endures for ever,
to him who alone does great wonders.
His love endures for ever.

Psalm 136, 1-4

Blessed are those who fear the Lord,
who walk in His ways.
You will eat the fruit of your labor;
blessings and prosperity will be yours.
Your wife will be like a fruitful vine
within your house;
your sons will be like olive shoots
around your table.
Thus is the man blessed
who fears the Lord.
May the Lord bless you from Zion
all the days of your life;
may you see the prosperity of Jerusalem,
and may you live to see your
children's children.
Peace be upon Israel.

Psalm 128

I lift up my eyes to the hills –
where does my help come from?
My help comes from the Lord,
the Maker of heaven and earth.
He will not let your foot slip –
he who watches over you will not slumber,
indeed, he who watches over Israel
will neither slumber nor sleep.
The Lord watches over you –
the Lord is your shade at your right hand,
the sun will not harm you by day,
nor the moon by night.
The Lord will keep you from all harm –
he will watch over your life,
the Lord will watch over your coming and going
both now and for evermore.

Psalm 121

The Lord is my shepherd,
I shall not be in want.
He makes me lie down in green pastures,
he leads me beside quiet waters,
he restores my soul.
He guides me in paths of righteousness
for his name's sake.
Even though I walk through the valley
of the shadow of death,
I will fear no evil,
for you are with me;
your rod and your staff,
they comfort me.
You prepare a table before me
in the presence of my enemies.
You anoint my head with oil;
my cup overflows.
Surely goodness and love will follow me
all the days of my life,
and I will dwell in the house of the Lord
forever.

Psalm 23

I love you, O Lord, my strength.
The Lord is my rock,
in whom I take refuge.
He is my shield and the horn
of my salvation, my stronghold.
I call to the Lord,
who is worthy of praise,
and I am saved from my enemies.

Psalm 18, 1-3

I cried out to God for help;
I cried out to God to hear me.
When I was in distress,
I sought the Lord;
at night I stretched out untiring hands
and my soul refused to be comforted.

Psalm 77, 1-2

I pray to you, O Lord,
in the time of your favor;
in your great love, O God,
answer me with your sure salvation.
Rescue me from the mire,
do not let me sink;
deliver me from those who hate me,
from the deep waters.
Do not let the floodwaters engulf me
or the depths swallow me up
or the pit close its mouth over me.
Answer me, O Lord,
out of the goodness of your love;
in your great mercy turn to me.

Psalm 69, 13–16

Answer me quickly, O Lord;
my spirit fails.
Do not hide your face from me
or I will be like those who go down to the pit.
Let the morning bring me word of your unfailing love,
for I have put my trust in you.
Show me the way I should go,
for to you I lift up my soul.
Rescue me from my enemies, O Lord,
for I hide myself in you.
Teach me to do your will,
for you are my God;
may your good Spirit
lead me on level ground.
For your name's sake, O Lord,
preserve my life;
in your righteousness, bring me out of trouble.

Psalm 143, 7–11

Your word is a lamp to my feet
and a light to my path.

Psalm 119, 105

When I consider your heavens,
the work of your fingers,
the moon and the stars,
which you have set in place,
what is man that you are mindful of him,
the son of man that you care for him?
You made him a little lower
than the heavenly beings
and crowned him with glory and honor.
You made him ruler over the works
of your hands;
you put everything under his feet.

Psalm 8, 3-6

May the peoples praise you, O God;
may all the peoples praise you.
Then the land will yield its harvest,
and God, our God, will bless us.
God will bless us,
and all the ends of the earth
will fear him.

Psalm 67, 5-7

Blessed is he whose help is
the God of Jacob,
whose hope is in the Lord his God,
the Maker of heaven and earth,
the sea, and everything in them –
the Lord, who remains faithful for ever.

Psalm 146, 5-6

I will exalt you, my God the King;
I will praise your name for ever and ever.
Every day I will praise you
and extol your name for ever and ever.
Great is the Lord and most worthy of praise;
his greatness no one can fathom.
One generation will commend your works to another;
they will tell of your mighty acts.
They will speak of the glorious
splendor of your majesty,
and I will meditate on your wonderful works,
and I will proclaim your great deeds.
They will celebrate your abundant goodness
and joyfully sing of your righteousness.

Psalm 145, 1-7

I know that the Lord is great,
that our Lord is greater than all gods.
The Lord does whatever pleases him,
in the heavens and on the earth,
in the seas and all their depths.

Psalm 135, 5-6

This is the day the Lord has made;
let us rejoice and be glad in it.

Psalm 118, 24

Sing to the Lord a new song,
sing to the Lord, all the earth.
Sing to the Lord, praise his name;
proclaim his salvation day after day.
Declare his glory among the nations,
his marvellous deeds among all peoples.
For great is the Lord
and most worthy of praise;
he is to be feared above all gods.
For all the gods of the nations are idols,
but the Lord made the heavens.
Splendor and majesty are before him;
strength and glory are in his sanctuary.
Ascribe to the Lord, O families of nations,
ascribe to the Lord glory and strength.
Ascribe to the Lord the glory due his name,
bring an offering and come into his courts.

Ps. 96, 1-8

List of Psalm texts

Picture Descriptions

Wash me, and I shall be whiter
than snow.

Psalm 51, 7